TEAM SPIRIT ®

SMART BOOKS FOR YOUNG FANS

THE DETROIT LIONS

BY
MARK STEWART

NORWOODHOUSE PRESS

CHICAGO, ILLINOIS

Norwood House Press
P.O. Box 316598
Chicago, Illinois 60631

For information regarding Norwood House Press, please visit our website at:
www.norwoodhousepress.com or call 866-565-2900.

All photos courtesy of Getty Images except the following:
Icon SMI (4, 14, 32), National Chicle (6, 16, 28), Bowman Gum Co. (7, 21, 25, 38, 40),
Black Book Partners (10, 14, 23, 31, 35 top right, 43 top),
Topps, Inc. (11, 18, 30, 34, 35 top left, 37, 42 both, 45), TCMA Ltd. (15), Exhibit Supply Co. (20),
Author's Collection (33), Salada Foods (35 bottom), Detroit Lions/NFL (39),
SCH Publications (41), Matt Richman (48).
Cover Photo: Icon SMI

The memorabilia and artifacts pictured in this book are presented for educational and informational purposes,
and come from the collection of the author.

Editor: Mike Kennedy
Designer: Ron Jaffe
Project Management: Black Book Partners, LLC.
Special thanks to Topps, Inc.

Library of Congress Cataloging-in-Publication Data

Stewart, Mark, 1960-
  The Detroit Lions / by Mark Stewart.
    p. cm. -- (Team spirit)
  Includes bibliographical references and index.
  Summary: "A revised Team Spirit Football edition featuring the Detroit
Lions that chronicles the history and accomplishments of the team. Includes
access to the Team Spirit website which provides additional information and
photos"--Provided by publisher.
  ISBN 978-1-59953-522-7 (library edition : alk. paper) -- ISBN
978-1-60357-464-8 (ebook) 1. Detroit Lions (Football
team)--History--Juvenile literature. I. Title.
  GV956.D4S76 2012
  96.332'640977434--dc23
                                        2012018316

Manufactured in the United States of America in North Mankato, Minnesota.
205N—082012

COVER PHOTO: The Lions get into a huddle on offense to call a play.

Table of Contents

ABOUT OUR GLOSSARY

In this book, there may be several words that you are reading for the first time. Some are sports words, some are new vocabulary words, and some are familiar words that are used in an unusual way. All of these words are defined on page 46. Throughout the book, sports words appear in **bold type**. Regular vocabulary words appear in ***bold italic type***.

Meet the Lions

There is an old saying in football that "defense wins championships." Fans of the Detroit Lions know this to be true. Great defense is what makes them stand up and cheer their loudest. That says a lot, because the Lions have had some great runners, passers, and receivers over the years.

The truth is that winning football games takes a full team effort. For more than 75 seasons, the Lions have been putting talented players on the field. When they work together as one, the results have been amazing.

This book tells the story of the Lions. They are similar to the animal they're named after. The Lions are a family, and they work as a team. Every year, their goal is to become the kings of the **National Football League (NFL)**. If their opponents lose focus for just an instant, they had better look out—the Lions will make a meal of them!

Quarterback Matthew Stafford has words of advice for his favorite target, Calvin Johnson. The Lions have had many great passers and receivers over the years.

Glory Days

In the early days of **professional** football, many of the best teams weren't part of the NFL. Instead, they were based in small cities where they were the "only game in town" for sports fans. The Portsmouth Spartans were just such a team. They played in southern

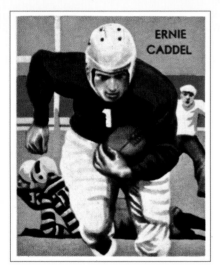
ERNIE CADDEL

Ohio, near the borders of Kentucky and West Virginia. The Spartans were very good—so good, in fact, that they were invited to join the NFL in 1930.

The Spartans nearly won the league championship in 1931 and 1932. They were one of the NFL's toughest teams. Coach Potsy Clark once decided he would use the same 11 players for all 60 minutes of a game against the Green Bay Packers. The Spartans won 19–0. The Packers had been the NFL champions the year before!

Portsmouth had a running attack that was almost unstoppable. Linemen Ox Emerson and George Christensen opened up holes for running backs Dutch Clark, Glenn Presnell, and Ace Gutowsky. Unfortunately for the people of Portsmouth, the **Great Depression** hit their city hard. In 1934, when fans could no longer afford to support the team, the Spartans moved to Detroit, Michigan, and became the Lions. A year later, they won the NFL championship.

The Lions built a dangerous offense during the 1930s and 1940s. Their stars included Ernie Caddel, Byron "Whizzer" White, Frank Sinkwich, and Bill Dudley. However, it was not until the 1950s—when the team's defense became *dominant*—that the Lions returned to the top of the NFL. Detroit played for the NFL championship four times during the *decade* and won the title three times. The defense starred Joe Schmidt, Les Bingaman, Jim David, Yale Lary, and Jack Christiansen.

The Lions of this *era* often looked to quarterback Bobby Layne for leadership. As long as there was time on the clock, his teammates believed he could guide them to victory. Layne got help from *dynamic* players such as Doak Walker, Cloyce Box, Hopalong Cassady, Bob Hoernschemeyer, Leon Hart, and Lou Creekmur.

LEFT: Ernie Caddel   **ABOVE**: Bobby Layne

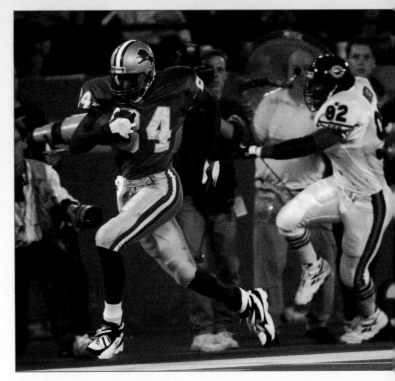

In the 1960s and 1970s, the Lions put many good players on the field. Their defensive stars included Alex Karras, Roger Brown, Wayne Walker, Mike Lucci, Lem Barney, and Dick LeBeau. Their top offensive players were Gail Cogdill, Nick Pietrosante, Greg Landry, Charlie Sanders, Mel Farr, Dexter Bussey, and Steve Owens. However, during these two decades, the Lions were never serious *contenders* for a championship.

By the 1980s, the Lions relied on the talents of an extraordinary running back named Billy Sims. He topped the **National Football Conference (NFC)** in touchdowns twice. In 1983, Sims helped the Lions win their first **division** crown in 26 years.

Detroit fans welcomed a new star when the Lions drafted Barry Sanders in 1989. Sanders was one of the fastest and most *elusive* runners in NFL history. He gained more than 1,000 yards 10 seasons in a row. With help from Herman Moore, Mel Gray,

LEFT: Barry Sanders
ABOVE: Herman Moore

Lomas Brown, Chris Spielman, and Jerry Ball, Sanders led the Lions all the way to the **NFC Championship Game** in 1991.

Six years later, Sanders had one of the great seasons in NFL history when he ran for 2,053 yards, caught 33 passes, and scored 14 touchdowns. He had another superb year in 1998 and needed just a few more yards to become the league's all-time leading rusher. Sanders surprised everyone by retiring, however. After a long career, he was just worn out. As the Lions entered the 21st century, the team and its fans prepared for "life without Barry."

Rebuilding an NFL team is no easy task. It takes good picks in the **draft** and good trades—and a little bit of good luck. In the years after Sanders retired, the Lions fell short in all three areas. In 2002, they took quarterback Joey Harrington with the first pick in the draft. Detroit surrounded him with talented young players such as Shaun Rogers, Kevin Jones, Dre' Bly, and Roy Williams. Year after year, the Lions began the season with high hopes only to drop to the bottom of the **standings**.

Detroit also turned to *veterans* such as James Stewart, Robert Porcher, and Jon Kitna. The Lions often played exciting football, but they were unable to return to the **playoffs**. In 2008, the team hit rock bottom. The Lions lost all 16 games they played.

Fortunately, this dark cloud had a silver and blue lining. The Lions began to pile up outstanding young talent. Calvin Johnson became one of the best receivers in the NFL. Ndamukong Suh brought a fierce new attitude to the Detroit defense. Quarterback Matthew Stafford returned from an injury to throw 41 touchdown passes in 2011. That season, the Lions went 10–6 and made it back to the playoffs.

Detroit fans have high expectations again. Winning in the NFL requires a balanced offense and a hard-hitting defense. The Lions are focused on building both, which means another championship is within reach.

LEFT: Roy Williams
ABOVE: Ndamukong Suh

Home Turf

For many years, the Lions shared a stadium with the Tigers baseball team. In 1975, they moved into a new indoor stadium called the Silverdome. It was located in the town of Pontiac, about 30 miles from Detroit. At the time, the stadium was the largest air-supported dome in the world.

In 2002, the Lions moved into Ford Field, which was named after the car company. The new stadium was part of the city's effort to revive its downtown area. It was built to include a 1920s factory, which gave the stadium an old-time feel. Ford Field was originally planned as an outdoor stadium. The city and the team later agreed it should be an indoor stadium instead.

BY THE NUMBERS

- The Lions' stadium has 65,000 seats and can expand to 70,000 seats.
- The stadium cost $500 million to build.
- The stadium has two huge video scoreboards. Each stands 27 feet high and 96 feet wide.

The view from the upper deck of Ford Field is breathtaking.

Dressed for Success

Detroit's colors are silver, blue, and white. The team has used them since 1934. Team owner George Richards let star runner and kicker Glenn Presnell and his wife choose the colors when the Portsmouth Spartans moved from Ohio. The Portsmouth uniform had featured a dark shade of blue. The Presnells' choice of a brighter shade of blue was inspired by the water in Hawaii. It is called Honolulu Blue and goes perfectly with silver.

In 1948, the Lions switched to maroon jerseys. The new color wasn't popular with fans. The Lions changed back to their old colors.

For many years, the Lions wore a plain silver helmet. In 1960, Detroit added a *logo*—a blue lion that looked like it was attacking its prey. Fans named the lion "Bubbles." It remains on the team's helmet today.

LEFT: Brandon Pettigrew wears the team's home uniform.
RIGHT: Yale Lary models the home uniform from the 1950s.

We Won!

During the 1930s, the **Western Division** of the NFL offered fans tough, hard-nosed football. Detroit shared the division with the Chicago Bears, Green Bay Packers, and Cleveland Rams (who now play in St. Louis). The Lions, Bears, and Packers still battle one another today in the **North Division** of the NFC.

"DUTCH" CLARK

In 1935, a year after they moved from Ohio, the Lions won the West by beating the Packers once and the Bears twice in their final four games. Detroit had a powerful running attack and a good defense. The Lions would need both against the New York Giants in the **NFL Championship Game**.

The teams met on a muddy field in Detroit. It snowed during the game, making the conditions even worse. The Lions didn't care. They jumped on the Giants early in the contest and won easily, 26–7. Four different Lions—Ace Gutowsky, Dutch Clark,

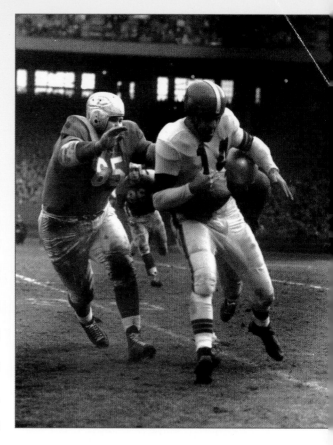

LEFT: Dutch Clark
RIGHT: Big Les Bingaman chases down Otto Graham of the Cleveland Browns in the 1952 title game.

Ernie Caddel, and Buddy Parker— scored touchdowns. Detroit celebrated its first championship.

The Lions next played for the NFL championship in 1952, against the Cleveland Browns. Parker had retired as a player and was now the Detroit coach. He built a great defense around Jack Christiansen, Yale Lary, and a gigantic lineman named Les Bingaman. Quarterback Bobby Layne led the offense. His favorite receivers were Cloyce Box and Leon Hart. Running back Bob "Horse" Hoernschemeyer was the key to the rushing attack.

As kickoff approached against the Browns, the Lions were feeling very confident. Several players were injured for Cleveland, while everyone was healthy for Detroit. Layne scored the game's first touchdown, and Doak Walker followed that with a thrilling 67-yard touchdown run. Meanwhile, the defense gave the Browns little room to move. The Lions went on to a 17–7 victory.

JOE SCHMIDT
LINEBACKER   DETROIT LIONS

The following year, the Lions added several talented **rookies** to their lineup. No one made a bigger impact than linebacker Joe Schmidt. He and his young teammates learned how to blend with the veterans as the season progressed. Detroit won its final six games to reach the 1953 NFL Championship Game.

Once again, the Lions faced the Browns. This time it was a very close game. The score was tied 10–10 after three quarters. Cleveland kicked two **field goals** in the final period to take a 16–10 lead. With less than five minutes left, Layne drove the Lions down the field. With the Browns expecting a pass to Hart, Layne fooled them with a touchdown toss to Jim Doran, who had caught only six passes all year. Walker kicked the **extra point** for a dramatic 17–16 win.

Four years later, the Lions won their fourth championship. New coach George Wilson led Detroit to a first-place tie in their division with the San Francisco 49ers. That set up a special playoff game between the two. The Lions beat the 49ers to earn a shot at the NFL title, once again against the Browns.

Detroit had revenge on its mind. In 1954, Cleveland had won the title in a blowout over the Lions. That loss still stung Detroit's players and fans. With Layne injured and unable to play, the Lions looked to Tobin Rote as his replacement. Rote was sensational. He threw for four touchdowns and ran for another.

The Lions also rolled on defense. Cleveland star Jim Brown had nowhere to run and gained just 69 yards. Detroit also pressured Cleveland passers into throwing five **interceptions**. The Lions led by 24 points at halftime and continued to pour it on in the second half. They won their fourth NFL title by a score of 59–14.

LEFT: Joe Schmidt
ABOVE: Yale Lary intercepts a pass against the San Francisco 49ers.

Go-To Guys

To be a true star in the NFL, you need more than fast feet and a big body. You have to be a "go-to guy"—someone the coach wants on the field at the end of a big game. Lions fans have had a lot to cheer about over the years, including these great stars …

THE PIONEERS

DUTCH CLARK   Running Back/Defensive Back/Kicker

• BORN: 10/11/1906   • DIED: 8/5/1978
• PLAYED FOR TEAM: 1931 TO 1932 & 1934 TO 1938

Dutch Clark had terrible eyesight, but that didn't stop him from becoming a star. When Clark carried the ball, he often faked his way past three or four defenders before he was brought down. Clark was one of the first players to wear gloves on cold days.

BOBBY LAYNE   Quarterback

• BORN: 12/19/1926   • DIED: 12/1/1986
• PLAYED FOR TEAM: 1950 TO 1958

Bobby Layne was famous for leading the Lions to one great comeback after another. Fans nicknamed him the "Blond Bomber" for his blond hair and strong throwing arm. In 1956, he became Detroit's kicker and made 68 percent of his field goals!

JACK CHRISTIANSEN　　　Defensive Back

- BORN: 12/20/1928　• DIED: 6/29/1986
- PLAYED FOR TEAM: 1951 TO 1958

When Jack Christiansen played, the Detroit defense was known as "Chris's Crew." Christiansen intercepted 46 passes during his eight seasons with the Lions. He also ran back eight punts for touchdowns.

YALE LARY　　　Defensive Back/Punter

- BORN: 11/24/1930　• PLAYED FOR TEAM: 1952 TO 1953 & 1956 TO 1964

Yale Lary could cover anyone in the NFL. He also had a strong and accurate kicking leg. Lary was the league's top punter three times.

JOE SCHMIDT　　　Linebacker

- BORN: 1/18/1932　• PLAYED FOR TEAM: 1953 TO 1965

During the 1950s, there was not a better linebacker in the NFL than Joe Schmidt. He was impossible to fake out and hard to block. Schmidt was voted **All-Pro** eight times.

ALEX KARRAS　　　Defensive Lineman

- BORN: 7/15/1935　• PLAYED FOR TEAM: 1958 TO 1962 & 1964 TO 1970

Alex Karras was a former wrestling champion who learned how to use his hands and arms to keep opponents from blocking him. Karras also had a knack for keeping his teammates loose with funny stories and jokes. He later became a television and movie actor.

LEFT: Bobby Layne
ABOVE: Jack Christiansen

MODERN STARS

DICK LEBEAU — Defensive Back

- BORN: 9/9/1937   • PLAYED FOR TEAM: 1959 TO 1972

During the 1960s, opponents threw the ball against the Lions at their own risk. That was because Dick LeBeau was waiting for them to try. He intercepted 62 passes in his career with the Lions. In 2010, LeBeau was voted into the **Hall of Fame**.

LEM BARNEY — Defensive Back/Kick Returner

- BORN: 9/8/1945   • PLAYED FOR TEAM: 1967 TO 1977

Lem Barney continued Detroit's great defensive *tradition*. During his career, he intercepted 56 passes and also returned kicks and punts. Barney was named to the **Pro Bowl** seven times in 11 seasons.

CHARLIE SANDERS — Tight End

- BORN: 8/25/1946   • PLAYED FOR TEAM: 1968 TO 1977

Charlie Sanders helped change the position of tight end. He could block on running plays and get open when the Lions needed to pass. Detroit quarterbacks looked for Sanders whenever the team needed to make an important first down.

BARRY SANDERS — Running Back

- BORN: 7/16/1968   • PLAYED FOR TEAM: 1989 TO 1998

Barry Sanders was the hardest player in the NFL to tackle. He led the NFC in rushing five times, including during the 1997 season when he gained more than 2,000 yards. He was voted the NFL **Most Valuable Player (MVP)** that year.

CALVIN JOHNSON   Wide Receiver

• BORN: 9/29/1985   • FIRST YEAR WITH TEAM: 2007

When Calvin Johnson joined the Lions, teammate Roy Williams nicknamed him "Megatron." That was because at 6′ 5″ and 240 pounds, Johnson played like a human Transformer. Johnson led the NFL with 1,681 receiving yards in 2011 and was named All-Pro for the first time.

MATTHEW STAFFORD   Quarterback

• BORN: 2/7/1988   • FIRST YEAR WITH TEAM: 2009

The Lions took Matthew Stafford with the first pick in the 2009 draft. His talent and toughness immediately made him a fan favorite. In 2011, Stafford became just the fourth quarterback in history to throw for more than 5,000 yards in a season.

NDAMUKONG SUH   Defensive Lineman

• BORN: 1/6/1987   • FIRST YEAR WITH TEAM: 2010

Ndamukong Suh was one of the scariest players in the NFL. When he took his position on the defensive line, opponents started looking for somewhere else to run. Few players in history have tackled ball carriers with more power or ferocity. He was voted Defensive Rookie of the Year in 2010.

ABOVE: Calvin Johnson

Calling the Shots

Long before anyone heard of Batman and Robin, the Lions had football's most famous "Dynamic Duo"—owner George Richards and head coach Potsy Clark. Richards was the man who moved the team to Detroit. He was also a radio pioneer. Thanks to Richards, fans across the country could listen to Detroit games on the radio.

The first coach that Richards hired was Clark. He had been a famous player in college, and he had also fought in **World War I**. With the Lions, Clark designed a record-breaking offense that was nicknamed the "Military Attack." He had a winning record every year he coached the team.

During the 1950s, Buddy Parker and George Wilson coached the Lions. Parker had some unusual players on his team. He recognized their *unique* skills and created new plays to take advantage of them. Parker was also good at finding ways to win when the Lions were behind in games. His players loved him for his never-say-die attitude.

Wilson took over from Parker and coached the Lions until 1964. He had been a star receiver for the Chicago Bears in the 1940s. His

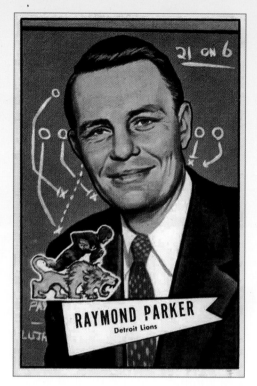

Buddy Parker led the Lions to a pair of NFL titles in the 1950s.

knowledge of passing helped Detroit build an excellent defense. The Lions went to the NFL Championship Game four times under Parker and Wilson.

Another star player who became a Detroit coach was Joe Schmidt. After retiring in 1966, he was hired by the Lions to coach their linebackers. He helped turn Mike Lucci into a star. Two years later, Schmidt became the team's coach. He was extremely strict, which made him unpopular with many of his players. They still played hard for him. In 1971, Schmidt led the Lions to the playoffs for the first time in 13 years.

One of the team's most interesting coaches was Wayne Fontes. Like Parker, Fontes experimented with new ways to use his best players. His "Silver Stretch" offense was very risky but also very exciting. In 1989, Fontes insisted that the Lions draft Barry Sanders. Fifteen years later, the legendary runner thanked his former coach in his speech when he entered the Hall of Fame.

One Great Day

Detroit fans weren't sure what to expect from the Lions as the 1991 season began. The team had finished at 6–10 the year before. However, with Barry Sanders and Chris Spielman leading the way, the Lions had the talent to beat any team—except on opening day. Detroit lost to the Washington Redskins, 45–0.

The Lions rebounded by winning their next five games. Unfortunately, all the news wasn't good. Several players—including quarterback Rodney Peete—went down with injuries. The worst was suffered by Mike Utley, one of the team's most popular players. In one terrible moment, he took an awkward hit and was *paralyzed* from the chest down. As doctors wheeled him off the field, Utley struggled to give his teammates the thumbs-up sign. The Lions were inspired and won their final six games to finish at 12–4.

That January, the Lions hosted their first **postseason** game since 1957. The Dallas Cowboys came to Detroit determined to stop Sanders. Detroit decided to cross up the Dallas defense. Backup

Mike Utley recreates his famous thumbs-up for reporters.

quarterback Erik Kramer hit Willie Green for a 31-yard touchdown. Then Melvin Jenkins intercepted a pass for the Lions and ran it back for another touchdown.

When the second half began, the Cowboys were still waiting for Sanders to strike. Instead, Kramer threw touchdown passes to Green and Herman Moore to put the Lions ahead by 25 points. Finally, in the fourth quarter, Detroit let Sanders do his thing. He took a handoff and darted through the Dallas defense for a 47-yard touchdown. That made the final score 38–6.

To this day, Detroit fans still talk about this amazing victory. They also celebrate the courageous way that Utley faced his terrible injury.

Legend Has It

Who was Detroit's best all-around player?

GLENN PRESNELL

LEGEND HAS IT that Glenn Presnell was. During the 1930s, the Lions used an offense known as the single-wing that made the most of three talented players—Dutch Clark, Ace Gutowsky, and Presnell. Clark handled the passing for the Lions, while Gutowsky did the hard running near the goal line. However, Presnell was the player who gave opponents nightmares. In 1933, he led the NFL with 1,296 running and passing yards. He kicked a 54-yard field goal in 1934 to set a record that stood until the 1950s. And in 1935, Presnell was the leading scorer on Detroit's championship team.

What was the best comeback in team history?

LEGEND HAS IT that it was Detroit's 1957 playoff victory over the San Francisco 49ers. That season, the Lions played San Francisco to see which team would move on to the NFL Championship Game. The 49ers took a 24–7 lead after two quarters and were celebrating in the locker room at halftime. This made the Lions angry. They stormed back in the second half to go ahead 28–27. The Lions stopped four drives in a row with an interception or by recovering a **fumble**. They added a field goal for an unforgettable 31–27 victory.

Which Detroit teammates performed on a number-one hit record?

LEGEND HAS IT that Mel Farr and Lem Barney did. In 1970, singer Marvin Gaye tried out for the Lions. He did not make the team, but Barney and Farr became his good friends. Gaye invited them into the studio when he recorded the 1971 hit song "What's Going On." Their voices can be heard in the background.

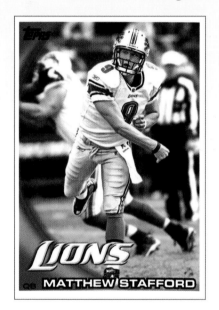

MATTHEW STAFFORD

When a team goes 2–14 during the season, its fans don't usually have much to cheer about. Or do they? Detroit fans are still talking about the day in 2009 when the Lions scored one of the most thrilling victories in team history—even though it was one of only two wins they managed the entire season. The game was played against the Cleveland Browns, just before Thanksgiving. It featured a showdown between two of the NFL's youngest quarterbacks, Brady Quinn of the Browns and Matthew Stafford of the Lions.

Things didn't begin well for the Lions. The fans at Ford Field groaned as Quinn threw three touchdown passes in the first quarter to give Cleveland a 24–3 lead. The Lions came roaring back. Stafford tied the score with three touchdown passes of his own—to Aaron Brown, Kevin Smith, and Calvin Johnson.

LEFT: Matthew Stafford
RIGHT: Calvin Johnson warms up before a game.

Detroit took the lead in the third quarter, but the Browns did not give up. They scored 10 points to move ahead 37–31. With less than two minutes remaining, Stafford led his team into Cleveland territory. On the last play of the game, he heaved a desperate pass into the end zone. The ball fell to the turf, but the Browns were flagged for **interference**. The Lions were given one more play.

Unfortunately, Detroit was now without Stafford. He had suffered a serious injury on the previous play. After the Browns called timeout to set their defense, a roar filled the stadium. Against all odds, Stafford trotted back onto the field. Wincing in pain, he fired his fifth touchdown pass of the day. Jason Hanson booted the extra point for a 38–37 victory.

"Matt's best play of the day," Detroit coach Jim Schwartz joked, "might have been eluding four team doctors to get back on the field."

Team Spirit

Every season, Detroit fans get to be part of one of the NFL's greatest traditions—Thanksgiving Day football. The Lions have hosted a game on this special day since 1934. Many of the team's greatest moments have come on "Turkey Day." Detroit's Thanksgiving game is broadcast on television and carried on radio stations all over the world.

Rooting for the Lions through thick and thin is another tradition in Detroit. Win or lose, the fans support their team. They stuck with the Lions even after their winless season in 2008. The team rewarded them three years later by returning to the playoffs.

Fans in Detroit never get tired of the team *mascot*, Roary, either. He's a big blue lion who leads the stadium in cheers. Roary has also been known to go waterskiing and snowtubing, and he rides mechanical bulls. He has become one of the NFL's most popular mascots.

LEFT: Chris Harris has a gift for a lucky Lions fan.
ABOVE: Fans bought this stadium pin during the 1950s.

Timeline

The Lions have given their fans a lot to cheer about over the years. This timeline shows some of the team's greatest achievements.

1934
The team moves to Detroit and becomes the Lions.

1949
Bob Mann leads the NFL in receiving yards.

1935
The Lions win their first NFL championship.

1940
Byron "Whizzer" White leads the NFL in rushing.

1953
The Lions win their second NFL championship in a row.

LIONS

DETROIT LIONS

FRONT ROW: Nussbaumer, Scout; Gandee, Walker, Karilivacz, Doran, Stanfel, Co-Capt.; Parker, Head Coach; Christiansen, Co-Capt.; Layne, David, Schmidt, Girard, Ramsey, Asst. Coach. 2ND ROW: Dr. Thompson, Kerbawy, Gen. Mgr.; Anderson, Pres.; Mains, Salsbury, Bibble, Long, Sewell, Cain, Martin, Middleton, McCord, Topor, Woit, Forte, Asst. Coach; Wilson, Asst. Coach. BACK ROW: Kelley, Trainer; Fucci, Campbell, Stits, Ane, Creekmur, Atkins, Miketa, Gilmer, Riley, Carpenter, Hoernschemeyer, Macklem, Mgr.; Erickson, Publicity.

This trading card shows the Lions in the 1950s.

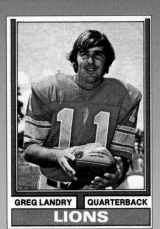

Greg
Landry

GREG LANDRY | QUARTERBACK
LIONS

Calvin
Johnson

1971
Greg Landry makes
the Pro Bowl.

1980
Billy Sims is voted
Offensive Rookie
of the Year.

2008
Calvin Johnson leads the NFL
with 12 touchdown catches.

1960
Gail Cogdill is named
Rookie of the Year.

1995
Herman Moore sets an NFL
record with 123 catches.

2011
The Lions return
to the playoffs.

Gail
Cogdill

Fun Facts

RUBBER BAND MAN

Matthew Stafford started wearing a rubber band on his left wrist for good luck around the age of seven. He still wears one today.

GOOD NUMBER

From 1967 to 1998, three all-time greats wore the number 20 for Detroit—Lem Barney, Billy Sims, and Barry Sanders. The Lions finally retired the number in 2004.

ACTING OUT

When Alex Karras was a boy, he wanted to become an actor like his dad. After his father passed away, he focused on football in order to get a college scholarship. After retiring from the NFL, Karras became a star all over again as—you guessed it—an actor!

ABOVE: Billy Sims was on   the great players to wear number 20 for the Lions. **RIGHT**: Eddie Murray

KICKING IT

From 1980 to 2011, Detroit had just two kickers, Eddie Murray and Jason Hanson. Murray was one of the most accurate kickers in NFL history. Twice he made more than 95 percent of his field-goal attempts. Hanson was known for his powerful right leg. He kicked 463 field goals in his first 20 seasons.

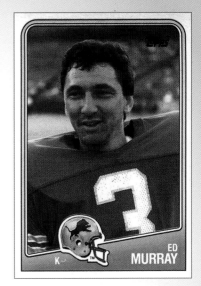

IT'S ABOUT TIME

In Detroit's 38–37 win over the Cleveland Browns in 2009, Matthew Stafford became the first rookie in 62 years to throw five touchdown passes in a game.

MANY HAPPY RETURNS

Through the 2011 season, six Lions have returned kicks for touchdowns of 100 yards or more—Terry Fair (105 and 101), Stefan Logan (105), Ron Jessie (102), Mel Gray (102), Billy Jefferson (101), and Pat Studstill (100).

JUDGMENT DAY

In the 1940s, Byron "Whizzer" White thrilled Detroit fans with his powerful running. In 1962, he became a *Supreme Court* Justice.

Talking Football

DOAK WALKER

"Bobby Layne never 'lost' a game. Time just ran out. Nobody hated to lose more than Bobby."

▶ **Doak Walker,** *on the Blond Bomber*

"You need to be responsible for your job on the field, and you have to be responsible off the field."

▶ **Matthew Stafford,** *on the pressure of being an NFL quarterback*

"I challenge my coaches almost as much as the players. I think that's my job as a head coach—to set high standards and to follow up all the time."

▶ **Jim Schwartz,** *on the quest for excellence*

"I'd rather run toward a defender than away from him. I'd rather watch him make the mistake than have me make it."

▶ *Dexter Bussey, on challenging opponents to make a tackle*

"He wasn't the fastest or the quickest, so he worked on being the smartest by studying receivers and **schemes**."

▶ *Charlie Sanders, on Hall of Fame teammate Dick LeBeau*

"I never expected to be able to do this. I'm just very thankful."

▶ *Barry Sanders, on running for more than 2,000 yards in a season*

"You always have to have faith things are going to get better."

▶ *Calvin Johnson, on turning a losing team into a winner*

LEFT: Doak Walker
ABOVE: Dexter Bussey

Great Debates

eople who root for the Lions love to compare their favorite moments, teams, and players. Some debates have been going on for years! How would you settle these classic football arguments?

The Lions of the 1930s would beat the Lions of the 1950s ...

... because they had too many weapons for any defense to handle. In the early days of the NFL, Dutch Clark was the league's most accurate passer. He led a team that included some of the greatest players of the day, including Ace Gutowsky, Glenn Presnell, Ernie Caddel, and Harry Ebding. Also, the 1935 championship team had the top-ranked defense in football.

LEON HART

Not a chance! The 1950s Lions would stop Clark and his teammates ...

... because their defense was even better. Joe Schmidt led a unit that had the league's toughest linemen and quickest defensive backs. Plus, how in the world would the 1930s Lions deal with Bobby Layne? He would complete passes to Leon Hart (   ), Cloyce Box, and Dorne Dibble all day long!

Charlie Sanders was the greatest pass-catcher in team history ....

… because he combined great hands with incredible toughness. During the 1970s, when Detroit needed a first down, everyone in the stadium knew the play: Sanders (RIGHT) over the middle. Almost every time he caught the ball, two or three defenders were waiting to tackle him. No one was better than Sanders at hanging on to the ball and stretching for a first down.

Not so fast! Calvin Johnson was Detroit's best receiver ....

… because no Lion has ever had his combination of size, speed, and skill. In his first five seasons with the Lions, Johnson caught 366 passes and scored 49 touchdowns. In 2012, no one was surprised when the Lions signed him to a new contract that made him the highest-paid receiver in the NFL.

For the Record

T he great Lions teams and players have left their marks on the record books. These are the "best of the best" …

Joe Schmidt

Mel Farr

LIONS AWARD WINNERS

WINNER	AWARD	YEAR
Frank Sinkwich	NFL MVP	1944
Don Doll	Pro Bowl MVP	1952
George Wilson	Coach of the Year	1957
Gail Cogdill	Rookie of the Year	1960
Joe Schmidt	NFL co-MVP	1960
Mel Farr	Offensive Rookie of the Year	1967
Lem Barney	Defensive Rookie of the Year	1967
Bubba Baker	Defensive Rookie of the Year	1978
Billy Sims	Offensive Rookie of the Year	1980
Eddie Murray	Pro Bowl MVP	1981
Barry Sanders	Offensive Rookie of the Year	1989
Wayne Fontes	Coach of the Year	1991
Barry Sanders	Offensive Player of the Year	1994
Barry Sanders	Offensive Player of the Year	1997
Barry Sanders	NFL co-MVP	1997
Ndamukong Suh	Defensive Rookie of the Year	2010

LIONS ACHIEVEMENTS

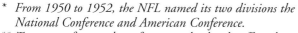

ACHIEVEMENT	YEAR
Western Division Champions	1935
NFL Champions	1935
National Conference Champions	1952*
NFL Champions	1952
Western Conference Champions	1953
NFL Champions	1953
Western Conference Champions	1954
Western Conference Champions	1957
NFL Champions	1957
NFC Central Champions	1983
NFC Central Champions	1991
NFC Central Champions	1993
NFC Wild Card Winners	2011**

* From 1950 to 1952, the NFL named its two divisions the National Conference and American Conference.

** Two teams from each conference make the playoffs each season as a Wild Card.

ABOVE: Barry Sanders, the 1997 co-MVP, loosens up before a game.
LEFT: Tobin Rote lets one fly against the Cleveland Browns in the 1957 title game.

Pinpoints

T he history of a football team is made up of many smaller stories. These stories take place all over the map—not just in the city a team calls "home." Match the pushpins on these maps to the **Team Facts**, and you will begin to see the story of the Lions unfold!

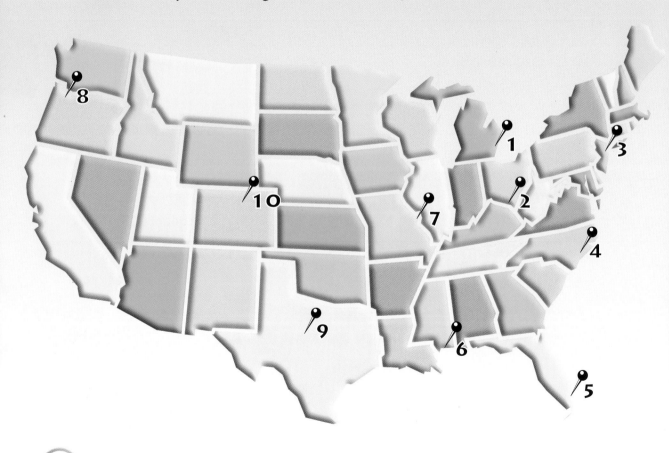

TEAM FACTS

1   Detroit, Michigan—*The Lions have played in the Detroit area since 1934.*

2   Portsmouth, Ohio—*The team played here as the Spartans from 1930 to 1933.*

3   Hopelawn, New Jersey—*Lou Creekmur was born here.*

4   Richlands, North Carolina—*Charlie Sanders was born here.*

5   Miami, Florida—*Lomas Brown was born here.*

6   Gulfport, Mississippi—*Lem Barney was born here.*

7   St. Louis, Missouri—*Billy Sims was born here.*

8   Portland, Oregon—*Ndamukong Suh was born here.*

9   Santa Anna, Texas—*Bobby Layne was born here.*

10   Fort Collins, Colorado—*Byron White was born here.*

11   Halifax, Nova Scotia, Canada—*Eddie Murray was born here.*

12   London, England—*The Lions played in the 1983 American Bowl* here.*

* The American Bowl was the annual NFL game played outside the United States from 1986 to 2005.

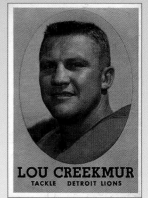

Lou Creekmur

Glossary

🧠 **ALL-PRO**—An honor given to the best players at their positions at the end of each season.

♣ *CONTENDERS*—People who compete for a championship.

♣ *DECADE*—A period of 10 years; also specific periods, such as the 1950s.

🧠 **DIVISION**—A group of teams that play in the same part of the country.

♣ *DOMINANT*—Ruling or controlling.

🧠 **DRAFT**—The annual meeting during which NFL teams choose from a group of the best college players.

♣ *DYNAMIC*—Exciting and energetic.

♣ *ELUSIVE*—Difficult to catch.

♣ *ERA*—A period of time in history.

🧠 **EXTRA POINT**—A kick worth one point, attempted after a touchdown.

🧠 **FIELD GOALS**—Goals from the field, kicked over the crossbar and between the goal posts. A field goal is worth three points.

🧠 **FUMBLE**—A ball that is dropped by the player carrying it.

♣ *GREAT DEPRESSION*—The economic crisis that started in 1929 and lasted until the 1940s.

🧠 **HALL OF FAME**—The museum in Canton, Ohio, where football's greatest players are honored.

🧠 **INTERCEPTIONS**—Passes that are caught by the defensive team.

🧠 **INTERFERENCE**—Illegally preventing a receiver from catching a pass.

♣ *LOGO*—A symbol or design that represents a company or team.

♣ *MASCOT*—An animal or person believed to bring a group good luck.

🧠 **MOST VALUABLE PLAYER (MVP)**—The award given each year to the league's best player; also given to the best player in the Super Bowl and Pro Bowl.

🧠 **NATIONAL FOOTBALL CONFERENCE (NFC)**—One of two groups of teams that make up the NFL.

🧠 **NATIONAL FOOTBALL LEAGUE (NFL)**—The league that started in 1920 and is still operating today.

🧠 **NFC CHAMPIONSHIP GAME**—The game played to determine which NFC team will go to the Super Bowl.

🧠 **NFL CHAMPIONSHIP GAME**—The game played to decide the winner of the league each year from 1933 to 1969.

🧠 **NORTH DIVISION**—A division for teams that play in the northern part of the country.

♣ *PARALYZED*—Unable to move a section of the body.

🧠 **PLAYOFFS**—The games played after the regular season to determine which teams play in the Super Bowl.

🧠 **POSTSEASON**—Another term for playoffs.

🧠 **PRO BOWL**—The NFL's all-star game, played after the regular season.

♣ *PROFESSIONAL*—Paid to play.

🧠 **ROOKIES**—Players in their first year.

♣ *SCHEMES*—Parts of a game plan.

🧠 **STANDINGS**—A list of teams, starting with the team with the best record and ending with the team with the worst record.

♣ *SUPREME COURT*—The highest court in the United States.

♣ *TRADITION*—A belief or custom that is handed down from generation to generation.

♣ *UNIQUE*—Special or one of a kind.

♣ *VETERANS*—Players with great experience.

🧠 **WESTERN DIVISION**—A group of teams that play in the western part of the country.

♣ *WORLD WAR I*—The war among the powers of Europe that lasted from 1914 to 1918. The United States entered the war in 1917.

OVERTIME

TEAM SPIRIT introduces a great way to stay up to date with your team! Visit our OVERTIME link and get connected to the latest and greatest updates. OVERTIME serves as a young reader's ticket to an exclusive web page—with more stories, fun facts, team records, and photos of the Lions. Content is updated during and after each season. The OVERTIME feature also enables readers to send comments and letters to the author! Log onto:

www.norwoodhousepress.com/library.aspx

and click on the tab: TEAM SPIRIT to access OVERTIME.

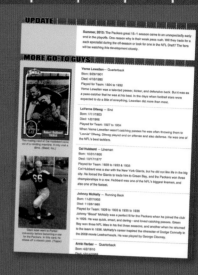

Read all the books in the series to learn more about professional sports. For a complete listing of the baseball, basketball, football, and hockey teams in the TEAM SPIRIT series, visit our website at:

www.norwoodhousepress.com/library.aspx

On the Road

DETROIT LIONS
2000 Brush Street
Detroit, Michigan 48226
313-262-2000
www.detroitlions.com

THE PRO FOOTBALL HALL OF FAME
2121 George Halas Drive NW
Canton, Ohio 44708
330-456-8207
www.profootballhof.com

On the Bookshelf

To learn more about the sport of football, look for these books at your library or bookstore:

- Frederick, Shane. *The Best of Everything Football Book.* North Mankato, Minnesota: Capstone Press, 2011.

- Jacobs, Greg. *The Everything Kids' Football Book: The All-Time Greats, Legendary Teams, Today's Superstars—And Tips on Playing Like a Pro.* Avon, Massachusetts: Adams Media Corporation, 2010.

- Editors of *Sports Illustrated for Kids. 1st and 10: Top 10 Lists of Everything in Football.* New York, New York: Sports Illustrated Books, 2011.

Index

PAGE NUMBERS IN **BOLD** REFER TO ILLUSTRATIONS.

About the Author

MARK STEWART has written more than 50 books on football and over 150 sports books for kids. He grew up in New York City during the 1960s rooting for the Giants and Jets, and was lucky enough to meet players from both teams. Mark comes from a family of writers. His grandfather was Sunday Editor of *The New York Times,* and his mother was Articles Editor of *Ladies' Home Journal* and *McCall's*. Mark has profiled hundreds of athletes over the past 25 years. He has also written several books about his native New York and New Jersey, his home today. Mark is a graduate of Duke University, with a degree in history. He lives and works in a home overlooking Sandy Hook, New Jersey. You can contact Mark through the Norwood House Press website.